JOURNEY

TO

NOAH'S ARK

Text by Ron Leadbetter,
Jerry Lemler and Russell Lemler

Photographs by Barry Rice and
Ron Leadbetter

LAKEMOOR PUBLISHING
KNOXVILLE, TENNESSEE

Copyright © 1998 by Lakemoor, Inc.

ISBN: 0-9651848-3-8

Library of Congress Catalog Card No.: 98-066467

Additional copies of this book may be ordered by calling or by visiting our website

Published and Distributed by:

LAKEMOOR PUBLISHING
P.O. BOX 506
KNOXVILLE, TENNESSEE 37901-0506

Telephone: (423) 577-2523
Facsimile: (423) 573-2032
Toll Free: (800) 390-8876

visit our website: www.lakemoor.com

Printed in the United States of America

TABLE OF CONTENTS

INTRODUCTION

Our odyssey to Noah's Ark in remote eastern Turkey was an arduous three-year effort in the making. It is almost certain that when you travel to such a dangerous part of the world, you can throw away your best constructed and most precise itineraries. You constantly improvise and merely go with the flow, while hoping and praying it carries you onward to your desired destination; and then back home again.

Then, there were times when we were completely at the mercy of 17 and 18 year old Turkish soldiers, who visibly brandished M-16 assault rifles in their boyish, smooth-skinned hands. We were, also, literally in the hands of our nameless drivers. Though they demanded to be well paid, (and they were, as there was no choice), we trusted them time and again to deliver us expeditiously, and more importantly, unharmed. We excused the former, as they repeatedly accomplished the latter. Thank you gentlemen.

On any trip of this magnitude, some arrangements inevitably go awry. We certainly had our share of such moments. On balance, though, we were extremely fortunate. As this book is being compiled, (Spring, 1998), we were, and possibly still are among the very last Americans to explore these ruins of a once great ship, though several other stateside expeditions have made the attempt. At least some have failed due to the overt escalation of hostilities in the area. Who knows when others will come along to see, to touch, to photograph, to sample or to investigate?

In the media, the four of us have been labeled "amateur explorers." While we don't perform explorations for a living, all of us were well-seasoned foreign travel veterans prior to departing Knoxville, Tennessee's McGhee-Tyson Airport for the first leg of our journey.

University of Tennessee attorney Ron Leadbetter had conducted numerous (and sometimes quite dangerous) foreign adventures that were avidly chronicled in newspaper accounts. A whitewater rafting enthusiast, he successfully negotiated the Zambezi River in Africa, and along with our traveling companion, Barry Rice, found himself amidst heavy bombing by Yugoslav Air Force planes in Croatia, shortly after the new nation declared its independence from the former Yugoslav state. Ron also, (along with Barry), was in Bulgaria for the first democratic elections to be held in that country in over 70 years, and attended demonstration rallies when the people rebelled against the Communists. Additionally, Ron has extensively traveled in Southeast Asia, exploring and visiting Vietnam, Cambodia, Myanmar (formerly Burma), Indonesia, Singapore, Hong Kong, and China.

Forensic psychiatrist and radio basketball commentator Dr. Jerry Lemler has several foreign travel credits of his own. Along with his son, Russell, he traveled the Mayan Trail through the Yucatan Peninsula of Mexico, and participated in the alien nation of Woodstock II in 1994. Jerry has visited the Greek Island of Santorini, and seen the rebuilding project of the once-great city of Thera, catastrophically vaporized by a colossal tsunami. He has also exchanged on-site pleasantries over tea with Turkish archaeologists excavating the ruins of Ephesus, and he stood on the stage where the Apostle Paul was nearly stoned to death by the Ephesians. Jerry also sat upon the very hill where Saint John was reputed to have written the Book of Revelations.

Private investigator Barry Rice is a true adventurer in every sense of the word. He has followed the ancient Silk Road from China to Istanbul, and, along with Ron, has been to Tashkent and Samarkand, Uzbekistan, the latter city being the center of Central Asian civilization during the 15th Century reign of Timur, (known to Westerners as "Tamerlane"). Barry visited Dracula's Castle in the Transylvanian town of Bran in eastern Romania, and, with Ron, has frequented Moscow and other Russian locations. Of special note is the fact that Barry has even climbed Africa's most famous peak, Mt. Kilimanjaro, in Tanzania.

West Point cadet Russell Lemler was a 17 year old high school senior on the Noah's Ark trip. Russell had previously climbed the ancient pyramids of Uxmal and Chichen Itza in Mexico. Additionally, he lived for awhile with a host family in Neuss, Germany as part of an exchange program. Together with his father, Jerry, Russell toured the ancient Russian village of Suzdal, and while in Moscow, he innocently sat in the back seat while his taxi driver led the militiamen (police) on a high speed chase through the city streets before finally being run down, apprehended, handcuffed, and taken away (car and all!) for driving recklessly while under the influence.

Yes, it's true, we had all been explorers. None of us, though, we assure you, in all our travels, had or ever have witnessed anything quite like what we wish to share with you now.

In this book about our October, 1996 excursion to the ark of Genesis fame, we make every effort, in both words and photographs, to take you along with us. We sincerely hope you enjoy the journey through the pages ahead.

* * * *

CHAPTER 1

And God Said Unto Noah. . .

In the Sixth Chapter of the Book of Genesis, we are told of God's disgust with the wickedness of humanity, and His resolve to destroy from the face of the earth all living beings. Yet, God was pleased with Noah, and chose to spare him and his family from the watery destruction planned for the rest of humanity.

Also, to be spared was a male and a female of each species of the animal kingdom, and seven each of certain beasts categorized as *"clean."* To Noah, God announced His intent to destroy civilization with a *"flood of waters upon the earth"* (Genesis 6:17, KJV [1]). Those not destroyed would ride out the deluge in a floating refuge of unprecedented proportions.

> *And God said unto Noah, The end of all*
> *flesh is come before me; for The earth is*
> *filled with violence through them; and,*
> *behold, I will destroy them with the earth.*
> *Make thee an ark of gopher wood; rooms*

---

[1]   King James Version.

1

shalt thou make in the ark, and shalt pitch it
within and without with pitch.

And this is the fashion which thou shalt
make it of: the length of the Ark shall be
Three Hundred cubits, the breath of it Fifty
cubits, and the height of it Thirty cubits.

(Genesis 6:13-15, KJV)

The rain came and the waters rose upon the earth, covering the hills and mountains, and destroying all not safely within the confines of the Ark.

And the flood was forty days upon the earth;
and the waters increased, and bare up the
Ark, and it was lift up above the earth.

And the waters prevailed, and were
increased greatly upon the earth; and the
ark went upon the face of the waters.

And the waters prevailed exceedingly upon
the earth; and all the high hills, that were
under the whole heaven, were covered.

(Genesis 7:17-20, KJV)

The Ark of Noah's salvation would not again touch

land until months after the rain ceased.

> *And the waters prevailed upon the earth a*
> *hundred and fifty days.* (Genesis 7:24, KJV)

> *And the waters returned from off the earth*
> *continually; and after the end of the hundred*
> *and fifty days the waters were abated. And*
> *the Ark rested in the seventh month, on the*
> *seventeenth day of the month, upon the*
> *mountains of Ararat.*

> (Genesis 8:3-4, KJV)

* * * *

CHAPTER 2

The Desire to See the Ark
by Ron Leadbetter

For many years I have been intrigued by reported efforts of various explorers to locate, on Mt. Ararat in eastern Turkey, the remains of Noah's Ark, which are described in the Biblical Book of Genesis. On occasion, an explorer would claim discovery of a splinter of wood or other evidence of the existence of the Ark of Noah, but reports of Ark findings were largely dismissed as bogus or unverifiable.

Several years ago I met Nashville amateur archaeologist Ron Wyatt in the Nashville airport upon his return to the United States from a brief period of captivity by Kurdish rebels in eastern Turkey. Before his capture, Wyatt and members of his family had spent a number of years exploring the countryside and examining what Wyatt believed to be the remains of the Ark in mountains several miles west of Mt. Ararat. The Turkish government was sufficiently persuaded that this area which has been called the "Duripinar site" contained the remains of Noah's Ark to plow a dirt road to it and construct a visitor's center. However, a military situation involving Kurdish separatists along with the Turkish government's reluctance to permit

4

foreign access have stymied further study of the site for several years.

Before Wyatt's arrival, I had an opportunity to scan a small paperback in which he outlined the evidence in support of his claim--evidence I found plausible, even persuasive. But my instincts as a lawyer assured a degree of skepticism. A brief documentary on the Discovery Channel whetted my desire to see the ruin firsthand. A fall 1996 trip to Russia and several southern neighboring republics of the former Soviet Union presented a golden opportunity to satisfy this desire. Tbilisi, the historic capital of the Republic of Georgia, lies some 150 air miles northeast of the Ararat region of eastern Turkey. It was here that I and traveling companion Barry Rice arranged to meet Jerry Lemler and his son, Russell, for an attempt to reach the reputed site of the Ark.

* * * *

CHAPTER 3

A Dangerous Part of the World
by Ron Leadbetter

The "Duripinar site" lies six miles from America-phobic Iran, and some 20 miles from Turkey's border with Armenia. Although the most direct route from Tbilisi to the Ararat region passes through Armenia, Turkey and Armenia are not on speaking terms. Barbed wire marks the line of demarcation between these hostile neighbors, and troops of both nations are stationed to prevent any breach of that line. A southern passage through hostile Iran is not possible for Americans. Therefore, we opted for a northern route crossing the Georgian-Turkish border at a newly opened border crossing between the Georgian village of Akhlatsikhe and the Turkish town of Ardahan before angling south to our destination.

While Turkey's hostile borders reveal the potential for violent warfare, this potential pales in comparison to the real, on-going violence that marks life within the present-day southeastern region of the sprawling nation. Much of southeastern Turkey, along with northern Iraq and western Iran, is populated by a huge Kurdish minority in an area referred to as Kurdistan. Within this region operate a number of violent "liberation" groups, seeking the

6

establishment of an independent Kurdish nation and/or the downfall of the present secular Turkish government. These militant groups desire to replace the elected government in Ankara with a fundamentalist Muslim state. [2]

Prominent among these groups is the fundamentalist Islamic Front, (known by the initials "IBDA-C/IKK" or "Islamic Great East Raiders-Front/Islamic Retaliation Detachments"), an Iranian-backed group. Even more violent is the Kurdistan Worker's Party ("PKK"), a Syria-supported separatist outfit responsible for some of the most ruthless terrorism in eastern Turkey in recent years. Since 1984, several thousand people have been killed in the fighting between the PKK and the Turkish troops seeking to establish security in southeastern Turkey with activities ranging from establishment of roadblocks, to placement of land mines, to kidnapping foreigners, including Americans. Ron Wyatt, himself, was kidnapped by Kurdish separatists several years ago, and escaped after a brief period of captivity. [3]

Dogubayazit is the city nearest to Mt. Ararat, and its main street blends images of the Old West with those of war footage from the evening news: Shepherds herd flocks of sheep down the middle of the street as a tank rumbles by in the opposite direction. Cattle, goats, donkey-pulled carts

---

[2] See photographs on page 51.

[3] See photographs on page 50.

7

and heavily loaded wagons pulled by young boys and old men share the same crumbling half-dirt/half-asphalt road with patrols of well armed Turkish soldiers, while old men in traditional garb sip tea at roadside tables. Only the occasional automobile or heavy truck added a sense of the ordinary to this otherwise incredible setting. During our Fall 1996 stay in the eastern city of Dogubayazit, the cool solitude of darkness was punctuated by the dull rumble of artillery fire in the distance, marking the evening's exchange between Turkish troops and PKK guerillas. An English language Turkish newspaper reported the deaths of 46 PKK terrorists in the region barely a couple of days after our departure. [4]

Our morning drive to the mountains east of Ararat served to explain why American and other foreign travelers are not seen in this part of Turkey. While dodging morning caravans of sheep, cattle and other livestock might prove attractive to some visitors, navigating numerous military roadblocks undoubtedly would not. Time and again, our group was halted at military roadblocks and subjected to inspections ranging from simple passport checks to open-trunk searches. [5]

Turning off the highway perhaps ten miles outside town, we drove for 15 to 20 minutes along a narrow dirt

---

[4] See photographs on pages 53 and 57.

[5] See photographs on page 52.

road winding into the sparsely populated, semi-arid mountains along Turkey's border with Iran -- and only 20 some odd miles from Armenia. [6] Rounding a curve, we came upon what I immediately recognized from a photograph in Wyatt's book as the visitors' center constructed by the Turkish government several years earlier. [7]

Because of the military conflict, the center currently stands idle and in a state of disrepair. Research activities in the vicinity ceased with Wyatt's capture by Kurdish separatists. Due to the hostile and precarious situation, Mt. Ararat and the "Duripinar site" are presently in a military restricted zone. The "Duripinar site" is (and was at the time of our visit) heavily patrolled by Turkish troops, and military outposts and roadblocks are prevalent throughout the region. The tense and dangerous military situation, combined with the Turkish government's refusal to permit foreigners to excavate the "Duripinar site", serve as ready explanations for the lack of scientific exploration of the first and greatest ship in recorded history. Pending a change in these conditions the mystery of the "Duripinar site" will remain largely undisclosed, save only for the minimal, inconclusive testing done to date and the photographic evidence within these very pages.

* * * *

---

[6] See photographs on page 62.

[7] See photograph on page 91.

CHAPTER 4

Admissible Evidence
by Ron Leadbetter

Parking alongside the visitors' center at the "Duripinar site", we emerged from our vehicle to see what surely must be one of the most unusual and fascinating sights on earth. A hundred yards below us sprawled a huge, elongated, boat-shaped structure far exceeding the length of a football field. More than 500 feet in length, the enormous earth-colored mound protruding distinctly from the surrounding terrain fits comfortably within Biblically specified dimensions. Incredibly, the physical dimensions of the formation are in all respects what one would expect if looking for the remains of the great gopher-wood vessel described in the sixth chapter of Genesis. [8]

Sheep graze peacefully in surrounding fields, and Mt. Ararat rises majestically to the north, as if exercising sovereignty over this remarkable scene. A small Turkish village is perched a stone's throw uphill from the site. [9]

---

[8]   See photograph on page 65.

[9]   See photographs on page 91.

10

Upon our arrival, Hassan, an elderly but energetic gentleman from the nearby village, who lives in the visitors' center and is referred to by locals as "Guardian of the Ark", extended us an enthusiastic greeting. Hassan was visibly excited at the prospect of having "real visitors" to show about his protectorate. Leading us down a steep hill, across rugged lava deposits from past volcanic activity in the area and onto the massive ruin of the Ark itself, Hassan allowed us to fully explore and photograph the site. For more than two hours our group clambered about the ruin, inspecting, photographing, and videotaping the site from every conceivable angle. [10]

Hassan took obvious pleasure in pointing out the small, spiral-shaped seashells on the boat-like formation, [11] and the four to six inch round entry point in the exposed south wall from which a 30-meter soil sample was taken by Ron Wyatt several years ago (yielding test results consistent with his Ark hypothesis). [12]

In fractured English, Hassan explained that the Ark was first spotted in a satellite photo in 1959. I later learned that Turkish Air Force Captain Ilhan Duripinar, hence the name "Duripinar site", while on a mapping

---

[10]   See photographs on page 64.

[11]   See photographs on pages 78 and 79.

[12]   See photograph on page 69.

mission, noted the presence of a large boat-shaped formation in the mountains south of Ararat. Subsequent earthquake activity exposed the western wall and further accentuated the boat-like appearance of the ruin.

Needless to say, if indeed it is the site of a vessel guesstimated to have been constructed in the Fourth Millennium, B.C., what is seen is a symmetrical form, rather than a wooden structure. Appearing anywhere else, this boat-like object would be nothing more than a puzzling oddity, as no such formations are reported to exist anywhere else in the world.

It is at least fortuitous that the "Duripinar site" is located in the mountains of Ararat, referenced in Genesis. The presence of such a geological quirk in the mountains of Ararat and nowhere else in the world surely demands careful scientific scrutiny, rather than summary rejection of the possibility that the final resting place of the Ark of Noah has been located.

Situated in the rugged mountains of Ararat at an elevation of more the 6,200 feet, there is no readily apparent reason for any boat other than the Ark of Noah to be resting in these mountains. The nearest body of water, Lake Vann, lies nearly 50 miles to the southwest, and the Black and Caspian Seas are a couple of hundred miles to the north. [13] Of considerable interest is the presence of tiny three-fourths inch long spiral seashells in the vicinity of the Duripinar formation. While it is theoretically possible a local scam artist trucked in and scattered about a load of seashells to enhance the mystery of the site, there is no evidence to believe that such occurred. Barring human tinkering, the presence of seashells at this unlikely elevation and location begs explanation, and more probably is related to the Genesis flood.

Resting at an angle approximately 12 degrees from horizontal, the Duripinar formation dramatically dominates the surrounding terrain. Little imagination is required to visualize a huge ship coming to rest, bow first, at the upper reaches of a sloping field in rugged mountains, settling at its current angle as flood waters receded. Alternatively, it is entirely plausible to imagine a ship swept down from higher elevations by a torrential lava flow, depositing the giant structure on its present perch, tilted toward Mt. Ararat and the valley between.

The massive exposed side wall of the boat form appears coated with black volcanic lava, while light colored soil has plainly fallen away from the wall, revealing its surface. The lava appears as a brittle coating, seemingly preserving the form from the ravages of wind and

---

[13] See map on page 45.

infrequent rain in this semi-arid region. [14]

The soil atop the site and within the perimeter of what appears to be remains of sidewalls forms an elongated central mound of dirt, sloping down from the center before rising again to meet the sidewalls. This appearance suggests the remains of an ancient ship, deck collapsed, partially buried by windborne sand, sculpted into its present form by the elements.

Limited geological studies of soil samples taken to date from the "Duripinar site" have yet to conclusively prove or disprove the formation as that of Noah's Ark. Without additional excavation any claim to the contrary is baseless. Yet, existing visible evidence challenges the skeptic who dismisses the possibility that the Duripinar formation is no more than a natural phenomenon.

That we had seen the Ark of Noah was the consensus of our group as we trudged back uphill to the visitors' center, turning one last time to behold the marvelous panoramic view featuring what quite possibly are the remains of the oldest manmade structure described in the Bible.

* * * *

---

[14]   See photograph on page 71.

CHAPTER 5

Crossing the Border
by Jerry Lemler

We were staying at 21 Gogibashvili Street in the capital city of Georgia when we drew up the final plans for the border crossing and the desired route to the Noah's Ark site. The day started for me a few minutes before 6:00 a.m. Not to wake Russell, I crept softly to the common bathroom down the hall, got dressed, and headed across the street with Ron, who had mirrored my movements, leaving Barry perfectly horizontal in the room they shared. Ron and I ascended the staircase to the fourth floor makeshift living room, where Ron flipped on the narrow, ancient television set, fine tuned it a time or two, and between the gray lines of snow and intermittent bolts of static, we conjured up the images of Bill Clinton and Bob Dole about to begin their first live debate of the 1996 general election campaign for president.

It was Monday, 6:00 a.m., Georgia time, but it was also Sunday, 9:00 p.m. in Atlanta. So, of course, we weren't in the stateside Georgian capital of Atlanta. We were, in reality, nearly half a world away, in the Republic of Georgia's refurbished, bustling capital city of Tbilisi. Specifically, we were staying in Elizabeth Haskell's hotel, known to one and all simply as Betsy's. Over the course of our three day stay in this simple, but nicely appointed 15 room hotel, we met any number of fascinating people. In the dining room, amongst the finely prepared and served meats, vegetables, cheeses, and wine, conversation was often light, and talk of home (America, England, Scandinavia) was lively. We were amongst expatriates and tourists from at least four continents, and I explicitly remember feeling like a Hobbit who had entered the last homely house on the left.

Our plans, formulated and revised time and again in the United States, called for us to take the shortest route possible. We had received appropriate warnings from our State Department, who informed us that although travel into this inflammatory part of the world was not strictly forbidden, neither was it especially encouraged. Simply put, we were on our own, though with our government's best wishes for a safe and productive journey. One particular conversation at Betsy's, however, on the evening before the Cleveland, Ohio presidential debate, altered our route of entry into eastern Turkey. We had not entirely anticipated the depth of the hostility that existed between neighbors, Armenia and Turkey. We had unwittingly and naively assumed we could pass through the border checkpoint between these nations without incident.

Betsy's was (and is) the place for the passing of updated and reliable travel information, what with so many of its guests coming and going with both business and holiday agendas. One couple, from Armenia, (unfortunately for them, but fortuitous for us), had recently returned to Betsy's Tbilisi retreat after having been turned away from this same border entry. They more than casually cautioned against our making the same futile crossing attempt, though it was by far the shortest, quickest, and most direct route. So Armenia was a "no go", and we took our barely two month old Turkish map which was already out-dated with the political and military realities of the region, and once again, drew up a new set of contingency plans. The alternate route would have us heading north, past the cheerful birthplace and childhood home of the beloved former Soviet dictator, Joseph Stalin, which we had visited two days previously.

Also, in traveling via this circuitous path, we would be sacrificing a significant chunk of time in getting to the reputed ark site; the northern trail to the newly-constructed border crossing added 150 miles of single lane dirt road to our journey.

Having said our good-byes over breakfast at Betsy's, we made the trek through the picturesque mountains of northern Georgia. As we neared the Georgian border village of Akhlatsikhe, the military surveillance began to assemble.

Twelve miles or so to the northwest of Akhlatsikhe,

amongst the scattered tanks and BDU-clad soldiers, we came upon the border crossing, menacingly bedecked with high-tech security cameras, and surrounded with a conspicuous ring of barbed wire. After proceeding through various inspectors, our driver deposited us at the rim of the crossing, where our bags would be searched for the first of many times over the next several days. There was nothing in our bags, as we knew, to arouse the slightest suspicion of even the most paranoid of guards. Yet, time and again our backpacks were searched, but revealed nothing more than our few personal hygiene items, some reasonably fresh pieces of fruit, and assortment of snacks including some "NEGRO" cookies, (I'm not kidding, that truly was their name for a popular Oreo-type edible in this part of the world), a couple of liters of bottled water, and, of course, our traveling papers, including our all-important yet easily obtained Turkish visas. To cross "no-man's land" between the Georgian and Turkish borders, we boarded an automobile that harkened back to a Detroit product of the late 60's. The driver cranked up the ancient machine, and for but ten dollars its four passengers were driven perhaps a hundred yards or so where our driver motioned us out.

We had arrived at our next stop; the newly constructed Turkish customs facility, reminiscent of a poorly stocked rest stop along the Pennsylvania Turnpike. There were no vending machines, no newsstands, no pay phones, no maps for sale, no clear plastic desk ornaments where snow could be stirred up by a shaking, and no taffy, not even of the Turkish variety. [15]

Our visas, passports, and, of course, our meager belongings were all thoroughly scrutinized by various border officials, who nevertheless stamped the documents, allowing us "safe" passage into the county. By this time (about an hour after leaving the Republic of Georgia), we were in northeastern Turkey, and though the nearest town, Ardahan, was only 70 miles to the west, we had no car, no driver, and thus no means of transportation. We anxiously searched for a rental car sign, but in the dirt strewn stretch of mountainous territory known as the new border crossing, alas, we found none. [16]

I am not often one given to an excessive belief in destiny, but I am hard-pressed on this occasion to label the emergence of one large (and in charge) gentleman who came to our aid at the remotest of Turkish outposts, anything other than heaven-sent. An immense figure of a man approached, looming over us without gesturing, thus clearly taking us by surprise. No one had spoken any English to us all day since we left the breakfast table at Betsy's, and while the massive olive-skinned man's enunciation hardly emanated from the academies of New Hampshire, it was as welcome an "Anglo" greeting as we

---

[15] See photograph on page 46.

[16] See map on page 45.

19

had ever heard.

"Where you go?", he inquired. Ron briefly unfolded the map he was holding, replying, "We're from America."

The large gent hardly seemed astonished by this revelation. Perhaps it was my Amelia Island shirt that had given us away. "Yes," he retorted, and asked a second time, "Where you go?"

"Tennessee," countered Ron. I reasoned at this point that the big man with the thick fingers would have surmised we were asking him how to get back to our beloved Volunteer state. To our great fortune he merely smiled instead.

"Where you need to go?", he queried, while looking at Ron's map. In another place and in another era, this question might have begged a story about some 8 by 10 glossy pictures with circles and arrows and a paragraph on the back of each one. This time, though, Barry placed his index finger directly on the Turkish town of Ardahan.

"Ah, Ardahan, yes, yes, I take you. You come with me!"

With a collective sigh of relief, we consented, leaving us with three questions of our own. "How, how much, and why?"

The broad-smiling Andre the Giant look-alike read the looks of puzzlement on our faces. With his meaty hands akimbo, like Steinbeck's Lenny, he replied, "I have a bus. I take you there. Room for you. No problem. Come with me." He gestured, pointing the way for us to clear yet another customs inspection.

With our visas now doubly stamped, our new acquaintance led us across a dirt lot to a grime-coated, chartered bus, with real seats and backrests, and an air conditioning unit that was noticeably gasping for its last breath.

"I take you to Ardahan," he repeated.

Instinctively, I reached for my wallet, but once again he anticipated my gesture, and motioned for me to stop.

"I am a Christian," he proudly exclaimed. "We are brothers. No money. We go to Ardahan together!"

If ever a prayer was answered, we felt as though a higher power had indeed intervened on our behalf. Literally stranded in the midst of a barren, hostile land and unable to speak any of the native tongues, out of nowhere comes this towering man with a bus, offering us safe passage to our overnight destination--a hotel in Ardahan. And, as his "brothers", he gives this to us at no cost!

The bus had a capacity of 32 people. The big man, it turned out, was leading a shopping tour group from Georgia across the width of Turkey, all the way to Istanbul. Counting himself, the bus had 28 Georgian passengers aboard at the border crossing.

Rejoicing, we took the last four seats, which were located in the back of the bus, whereupon we were instantly offered a fine variety of fruits to munch on by our fellow passengers, none of whom could speak a word of English. It took a minimum of two hours in the sweltering afternoon sun for our "tour director" to process the group's entry papers, and so we sat, and ate, and perspired, and ate some more.

Meanwhile, after we had been aboard the bus for an hour, and with no readily apparent discernible cue, the singing and dancing began. Some of the shoppers had strung a row of four hanging salamis across the bus's ceiling. As they dangled precariously downward, the swinging mobile salami stalactites seemed to provide a perfectly natural projectile adornment for dancing in the aisle. [17]

---

[17] See photograph on page 47.

Someone turned on a cassette tape recorder, and as if they had been painstakingly choreographed, the revelers performed in unison to the genuine up-beat Georgian folk dance tunes coming out of the portable machine.

One woman in particular, a rather wide one at that, came down the aisle and approached us. She gestured for us to join her in a contortion of sorts, but before any of us could decline her invitation, a new tune began playing, the wide woman turned back around, and she started leading the others in full-throated song. Had we only known the words, we would have gladly joined in, but alas, it did not even faintly resemble "Louie, Louie." We ate figs, instead.

At last, the beneficent large man boarded the bus, and by late afternoon, we were off to Ardahan. I turned to Barry and said, "This is it. We're actually on board the second coming of the Magical Mystery Tour!" And, you know, in a way, we were.

* * * *

CHAPTER 6

The Interrogations of the
"Knoxville Four"
by Jerry Lemler

As it turned out, our bus was the first of two such vehicles headed for the majestic city of Istanbul. This great metropolis of ten million inhabitants, part in Europe, part in Asia, divided into two by the Bosphorus River, was to be the final destination on our own tentative itinerary. I suppose the large man and his troupe of shoppers, singers, and dancers would have kindly given us a ride all the way there had we so desired, and, momentarily, we gave the notion some thought; but only briefly. We still had an ark to find, (hopefully), and so we opted to depart the bus 78 miles down the road, once it arrived in Ardahan. And, it only took us another four hours to get there!

The single lane, dirt road meandered around and through the hills and mountains of eastern Turkey, as our bus kicked up copious amounts of sand and rocks along the way. The floor show was winding down, while Barry and Russell nodded off into dreamland. Not for very long, though. Our driver and his giant up-front traveling companion soon realized we had not only out-paced the second bus, but we'd lost it completely. We stopped near some farm shacks and an old drinking well to allow time for the trailing bus to catch up and meet us. So, we waited, and waited, and waited some more.

Yes, the vast scenery was eerily beautiful, and the well was, well, interesting. But there are only so many partial conversations to be had with the curiosity-seeking local farmers and shepherds who had come down the hillside to greet us. Even they grew weary of the novelty, as over two hours passed and the sun set, though not another vehicle came into view from either direction.

Word eventually passed through the crowd, (we never learned by what means), that the second bus had broken down. This made perfect sense to me, and since we hardly had any alternative options, we did what by now we had learned to do best--we waited some more. With its compressor fixed, the second bus, marked only in the distance by a glimmering pair of headlights, finally trudged its way up the steep hill in the dark, and once again we were ready to roll on to Ardahan.

It took yet another hour for us to reach the town itself. Most of us were asleep, the singing and dancing but a distant border memory, and the refreshments long ago having been gratefully consumed. Our driver pulled the mighty caravan to a stop along a dimly lit cobblestone street, and the portly Christian gentleman motioned for us to leave his gracious presence.

We bade our tour group farewell, most of whom barely mumbled their unintelligible benedictions to us, as we stepped out into the Ardahan darkness. We hardly had time enough to wipe the sleep from our eyes. As we gathered ourselves and stepped into the decidedly cool nighttime October air, not 50 yards up the cobblestone street we came upon an "Otel" sign. In response to Ron's inquiry, "Hotel?", three young Turkish men lounging nearby led us into an ordinary appearing two story building.

Before we would learn that we'd be staying the night, we were herded down a short, dark corridor and then up a menacingly narrow flight of stairs. This was billed as an "otel", but at the top of the stairs our view was unlike that of any "Triple A" recommended facility we had ever seen. It was akin to being on Baltic or Mediterranean without having rolled doubles. What would be our nighttime accommodations basically resembled a small, one bedroom flat, and not a particularly desirable one at that.

Our hosts were gathered in what appeared to be the hotel's main room, and they pointed to a lumpy sofa, indicating we should sit down. Ron sat in a chair by himself across the way, while Russell sandwiched himself between Barry and me on the sofa. We soon learned we were the only guests to be spending the night at the unnamed hotel, and word of our arrival spread quickly to the local authorities.

The four young Turkish "proprietors" of the establishment were certainly affable enough. The three men nervously crisscrossed the room constantly. Their ubiquitous presence in the crowded hotel lobby was easily noted, as they scurried back and forth to quickly and quietly answer and make calls on the unmarked rotary phone. Our lone female host, who somewhat resembled tennis star Steffi Graf, graciously served us tea and Turkish coffee, the latter being very dark and equally strong. [18]

Within five minutes, the friends of our hosts began to arrive. Amongst the first batch was a man who of course spoke no English. After a few minutes of playing the well-worn game of "Why are you here?", and "Where do you want to go?", he agreed to drive us the next day to the southeastern Turkish town of Dogubayazit. The man pointed to his watch and held up six fingers. He grunted, to indicate he would return for us at six in the morning. We noted it was already closing in on 9:30 p.m. It would be a short night, indeed.

No more than 15 minutes after our arrival, a heavy thump, thump, thump on the stairway heralded the emergence of nine or ten machine gun toting members of

---

[18]   See photograph on page 48.

the local Turkish security force. These were clearly the no-nonsense guys and one no-nonsense young lady. Their leader, a tall, thin fellow of about 35, was suitably dressed in a black trenchcoat from which the pocket bulge of a revolver could unmistakably be seen.

He and his assistants made a series of short telephone calls. We could not make out exactly what was being said or decided, but the conversations certainly related to our unexpected arrival. After thoroughly searching the premises, which of course didn't especially take too long, they interviewed our female host, "Steffi". I'll tell you now they weren't discussing her highly renowned forehand. Finally, they approached us, and to our surprise the commander spoke enough English to be understood.

He inquired of us as to why we had come in the middle of the night to Ardahan, whereupon we replied we were simply tourists. Naturally, the commander asked for our passports, and he carefully thumbed through all four. One by one, as he called out our names, we identified ourselves to our inquisitor. Each time, he nodded and then returned our documents. Satisfied we likely weren't Kurdish sympathizers and we possessed no contraband, he wished us well and snapped his fingers loudly, whereupon his entourage, with the boss in the lead, descended the stairs and left the hotel.

It had been a very long day, full of several highs and lows, and more than a casual scare or two. We were quite tired, and so we excused ourselves and went into our hotel's only bedroom. It was a humbly equipped squarish cubicle with three single beds lined up in a row, side by side. It looked like one of us would have to sleep on the floor, but before we could draw straws, our hosts carried in the lumpy sofa from the lobby. Thankfully, Barry opted for an evening on the couch.

The bathroom was down a short hallway near the head of the stairs. While it did have cold running water, the toilet was merely a hole the ground; and I must confess, a not particularly clean one. The bedroom was decidedly cold, and so we took off only our shoes. Yes, we slept in the very same clothes we had dressed in earlier (much earlier) in the morning at Betsy's. The room had no windows, but a foot square piece of cardboard had been mounted on one wall, covering a vent through which, paradoxically, cool air was blowing. As we lay in the dark our minds were racing with thoughts of all we had done this day, and with hopes of a promising day ahead.

Then Ron uttered a most prophetic piece of advice. "Keep your passports handy, where you can find them," he cautioned. The seemingly endless day was capped off just before midnight, as the door to our room was thrown open and three immigration officials barged in. One of them flicked on the single electric light bulb overhead, while another, speaking in very understandable English demanded, as Ron had foretold, to see our passports, yet again. Finding them in order, he too wished us well, and departed. At long last we fell asleep in the hotel with no name.

* * * *

CHAPTER 7

Dogubayazit or Bust
by Jerry Lemler

We left our no-name (and no frills) hotel in Ardahan as planned at 6:00 in the morning of Thursday, October 10, 1996. After our interrogation at the hands of the Turkish security forces the night before, interrupting our preparations for sleep, we were most relieved to see the rising morning sun. Our destination was the southeastern border town of Dogubayazit, where we hoped to be deposited near the reputed remains of the great Ark of Noah.

Crammed along with our driver into a compact "taxi", our four hour ride south to the Ararat region was decidedly scenic, though after considering what we had been through already, largely uneventful. We divided our thoughts between relief at having gotten out of Ardahan intact, and anticipation over the possibilities laying ahead, as the seemingly endless, tortuous paved highways stretched out before us. Every so often the four of us rotated positions in our "taxi", so that no one was permanently relegated to the terribly uncomfortable hump-straddling middle rear seat. Instead of dirt, at times the roads we traveled were pot-holed pavement, and we were duly warned about the likelihood of encountering a flat tire. [19]

With his lucky prayer beads dangling from the rear view mirror, our driver, who spoke next to no English, did manage to entertain himself, (if not us), by playing some all-too-repetitious vernacular music on his modified tape player. It sounded something like Habib's Greatest Hits, as I recall. [20]

The city of Dogubayazit more than aptly exemplifies the phrase, "slice of life". The popular Fodor's describes this extreme eastern Turkish metropolis as a "frontier town". Their description may be overly kind.

In reality, spending the better part of two days in and about Dogubayazit was itself truly one of the unexpected enjoyable highlights of the entire odyssey. Our driver took us to a couple of hotels on the outskirts of town, where Ron went inside seeking assistance in locating the alleged ark site. On both occasions, he came away empty-handed and somewhat disillusioned. Not only did he fail to provide us with safe passage to the ark, he was bewildered to learn that no one in town seemed to have a glimmer of recognition of what he was talking about. Naturally, though, Ron was offered rooms for the night,

---

[19] See photograph on page 49.

[20] See photograph on page 52.

which he graciously rejected.

We had not yet completely lost hope, though personally I was close to it. In our despair, Barry proved why he is the ultimate private investigator, though his tenacity did not payoff at the local police station. Led by the sleuth's perseverance we went into Dogubayazit's police headquarters, though no one recognized our sketching of an ark. The official protectors of Dogubayazit were friendly enough, though they spoke little to no English. We gestured, played a none-to-shabby game of charades, and tried various forms of pantomime with the police officers, all to no avail. Ron took out a hand drawn sketching of the ark remains, but none of the officers gave even the slightest sign of recognition or understanding. They either had never heard of Noah's Ark, or they were not going to tell us about it. [21]

At this juncture, we were lost and utterly dejected. It appeared as though the central and dominant focus of our journey nearly halfway across the globe would end in absolute futility. We would have to settle for an up-close picturesque viewing of Mt. Ararat itself, and no more.

Once again, Barry relentlessly prodded us onward, as he said "Watch me, fellows. This is what I do for a living." He was firmly resolved to not leave eastern

---

[21]   See photograph on page 54.

Turkey until he had interrogated every last man, woman and sheep in Dogubayazit. He would not be deterred.

With our driver growing weary and anticipating his none too paltry three hundred American dollars ($300.00) fee, Barry pointed him toward what appeared to be a newly constructed edifice on the main street of Dogubayazit, the Hotel Ortadogu.

The four of us got out of the car and entered the glass and stainless steel modernistic lobby of the Ortadogu. The desk clerk, a young friendly chap, (who doubled as our gregarious waiter later at dinner), spoke but ten words of English. Appropriately enough, they were: cola, water, tea, hotel, room, shower (we were most appreciative of this one!!), chicken, lamb, no, and problem. Though he was unable to interpret our "ship on a mountain", he was insightful enough to summon the hotel manager to assist us. The finely attired manager, ever so proud (and rightly so) of his new facility, was fluent enough in conversational English to reach down into a drawer beneath the front desk and show us a rather worn, yet unmistakably recognizable sketch of the great boat. It matched Ron's drawing perfectly. We had, at last, hit paydirt!! [22]

The arrangements were simple enough. We agreed to stay the night at the plush Ortadogu (ten dollars for a

---

[22] See photograph on page 55.

single--breakfast included), and the manager consented to procure a driver to take us to the ark site the following morning.

We were the first Americans to ever stay in the new hotel, and by eastern Turkish standards the accommodations were better than first class. The elevators were not operational, so we trudged up the three flights of stairs with our bags to our respectably furnished row of rooms. Ten dollars apiece got us four separate single rooms, and though I loved my son very much and I certainly enjoyed the company of my friends, after being crammed into the back of a Georgian tour bus, a tiny room in Ardahan, and a compact car for hour upon hour with these guys, I welcomed the chance, even for one night, to have a room to myself. I gladly handed over a ten dollar bill.

Our rooms were sizeable, and offered a bird's-eye view of the main street of Dogubayazit. A porch, large enough to sit on, displayed Mt. Ararat as though you were walking into a diorama. Best of all, the bathroom had a shower with a few drops of warm water, and it contained the first commode I had seen in a couple of days.

I unpacked the few items remaining in my backpack, took a couple swigs of my ever-present bottled water, and spent a richly deserved, self-indulgent hour in my own private bathroom. Afterwards, I sat out on my porch to soak in some of the day's diminishing sunlight. People and animal watching in Dogubayazit resembled a carnival in motion right before my eyes. [23]

Continuously passing by on the street below came groups of sheep, some tended in flocks, with a few having gone AWOL (absent without official leave). Next came a Turkish armed military tank, followed by a team of oxen. The dusty street then gave way to a young man on a Harley, who passed a small herd of cattle. The bustle and noise of an afternoon of commerce in Dogubayazit was infectious and invigorating. The four of us gathered in the lobby, and took a pleasant late afternoon promenade around the town.

We came back to the hotel in time for dinner, and I guess word had not yet infiltrated eastern Turkey about the Ortadogu's fine cuisine. As the only diners in the room, we were not required to make reservations. The young desk clerk transformed himself into our waiter, and he politely asked if we desired chicken or lamb as the chef's selection for an entree.

With the day's many activities behind us, we were ravishingly famished. We all chose to have both the chicken AND the lamb. When your entire vocabulary is limited to but ten words, and "and" is not amongst them,

---

[23] See photograph on page 56.

it makes such a routine matter as ordering a meal next to agonizingly impossible. To his credit, of course, our waiter spoke more English than we did Turkish.

Then, in what could best be described as a prototypical Abbott and Costello dialogue, each member of our vagabond party received either chicken or lamb, but not both. Additionally, having cased the town that afternoon, we realized there were no local fast food establishments to satisfy our lingering hunger pangs. So, we devoured several plates of various breads and cheeses, downed a few "colas", and eventually retired to the lobby, where we idled the evening away with the first game of "Boggle" ever played in Dogubayazit, Turkey.

No matter that all of us were awakened by the repeated dull thumping of artillery shells exploding in the distance, and the piercing 5:00 a.m. cries of muezzins (Muslim clerics) from the electronic amplifiers of the towering minarets of the local mosques. Though we never saw the advertised gymnastic facilities, I'll tell you now, the Ortadogu is THE place to stay if you are ever in the vicinity of Dogubayazit.

* * * *

CHAPTER 8

From a Younger Perspective
by Russell Lemler

Being the first American teenager [24] to walk upon the vestiges of Noah's Ark was a rare and special occasion for me, and one I am most unlikely to ever forget. My journey through foreign lands appears in my memory as a collection of chaotic events; the focal point of these images is the Ark. In retrospect, the trip was a rush of excitement and high-speed travel, with the exception of the two hours spent on the Ark. When I stood at the crest of the site and looked out to the snowy peak of Mt. Ararat, there were no bustling bazaars, crazed taxi drivers, or streets full of milling goats. It was quiet. We may have just passed a few military posts and some armed guards, but the Ark itself was an isolated system of peace, where I could observe and reflect. When it was time to leave, I realized that I should not be the last American teenager to witness the grandeur.

I have cherished those times in my life when I've been able to learn about my fellow man, both present and

---

[24] We are unaware of any other American teenager having ever visited this site.

past, by first-hand exploration. In particular, I have been especially drawn to our ancient forbearers. Spending the summer of 1994 at the Crow Canyon Archaeological Center in Cortez, Colorado enabled me to feel a kinship with our Native American citizens, some of whose descendants became, and are still my friends. I am equally thankful that I've been fortunate enough, on two occasions, to explore the ancient ruins of Chichen Itza in Mexico's Yucatan Peninsula. Other excursions to Uxmal and Kabah offered me additional perspectives on the noble Mayan culture.

The primary difference between my observations at the Ark and those I made at other sights is tourism. My father has a photograph of me at Chichen Itza, and in the background are hundreds of foreigners experiencing the Mayan legacy. In contrast, my pictures from the ark show me standing amongst ordinary dirt, or next to a goat. I certainly enjoyed and appreciated the serenity of the ark site, but I am saddened by the fact so few have explored it for themselves.

Yes, I have been privileged to stand upon the vastness of the Ark of Noah. Of far greater import, though, than one person's journey, no matter how momentous it may be, is to leave behind, as it were, a trail of bread crumbs. May this book be a pathway for others.

* * * *

39

CHAPTER 9

Reflections and Afterthoughts
by Jerry Lemler

All four of us have stood before church groups and civic organizations in the last year and a half since returning from Turkey. We have passed around a piece of one of the ballast stones, and shared some of the seashells we brought back with us. Inevitably, we are asked two questions about our journey. They are, "Is it really Noah's Ark?", and "How did it feel to be on the oldest and most famous ship in the recorded history of the world?"

These have not exactly been easy inquiries for us to offer simple, routine explanations. In retrospect, though, we give you the following as our best responses.

We truly stood upon what appears to be the remains of an enormous, ancient boat, lying on a slope atop a 6,200 foot barren mountain landscape in the shadow of Mt. Ararat in eastern Turkey, where by any account other than Genesis, it doesn't belong. No water of any kind, fresh or salt-laden, exists for many miles in any direction, and yet numerous, tiny, delicate white seashells abound on and around the boat remains. It is certainly not as if these shells were planted in anticipation of our arrival.

Unlike at home, no entrepreneurs are busy at their drawing boards making preparations to develop a "Noah's Ark" themepark. In fact, as we have noted, tourists and would-be explorers from the west are generally excluded from the site by the Turkish government.

Our route was long and circumferential. Our interrogations were not especially of the friendly, "nice to see you", kind, and we repeatedly had to show our passports and empty out our bags for patrol units at numerous checkpoints. We were shaken from sleep by artillery shells blasting through the night, and we could not determine whether they were incoming or outgoing.

Approaching the recent discovery, we did not believe we were cynical, but we did hold onto a share of healthy skepticism. We supposed this led to a desire on our part to confirm or refute the site as evidence of Genesis "on the spot". Accordingly, for the first hour or so we eagerly abounded the ship, from Russell saying, "Hey, Dad, look at these shells!", to Barry, standing in amazement while inspecting what he knew to be one of several of the ship's ballast stones. Within that hour we knew we were standing on an ancient boat of Brobdingnagian [25] proportion.

---

[25] A reference to the Land of the Giants in Swift's book *Gulliver's Travels*.

We saw, felt and set foot upon what we believe to be Noah's Ark. Additional proof cementing this belief arose from the fact that the skeletal remains most assuredly came to rest, as was told in the Biblical Book of Genesis, in the "mountains of Ararat."

Then we were struck by a sensation of awe. We became believers, and marveled at how Noah, or anyone else for that matter, could have physically constructed such a massive floating vessel with the limited engineering skills and primitive tools available to a man only nine generations removed from Adam and Eve. Amazed, exhilarated, and privileged were some of the feelings we keep to this day regarding the events of the morning of October 11, 1996.

We hope that you, the reader, can now share some of these same feelings with us. Mankind and womankind thirst for legitimate evidence of our spiritual roots, and delight in its discovery. We also yearn for new sources of conviction to bolster the old bastions of our faiths, whatever form they may take. The Judeo-Christian creed is ever judged against, and not found wanting by its high standards of credibility. In the case of Noah's Ark, I believe these standards were indeed once again measured, and were not found in any way to be deficient.

* * * *

CHAPTER 10

Photographs of our Journey

When we were exploring the boat-like formation in the mountains of Ararat, we were not taking photographs for the purpose of writing a book. It was nearly a year after we came back home when we decided to prepare a written and pictorial account of our journey. Some of the pictures that you will see were retrieved from videotapes; therefore, the quality of these pictures may not be as good as regular photographs.

A map, not drawn to scale, has been included on page 45 to show the general part of the world in which the mountains of Ararat are located. In addition, some of the cities we visited on our trip to the "Duripinar site" are noted on the map.

We now present for your inspection photographic documentation of our journey from the Georgia-Turkey border crossing to the town of Ardahan, then to Dogubayazit (a city close to Mt. Ararat), and finally, what we saw in the mountains of Ararat - intriguing evidence that cannot lightly be dismissed!

So, is it a rock formation, or clay upthrust in a field of lava, as some have opined. . . or is it the Ark of Noah?

There will be no further testing of the "Duripinar site" pending a cessation of hostilities in the region and a relaxation of the restrictive ban imposed by the Turkish government on scientific exploration by non-Turkish investigators. In the meantime the mystery of the site remains unsolved and open to debate. What do you think? Look now, and, judge for yourself . . .

Our journey can be followed on this map (which is not drawn to scale). We began in Tbilisi and then travelled across the Georgia-Turkey border to the town of Ardahan. After spending the night there, we then travelled to the city of Dogubayazit, where we had a difficult time determining the exact location of the reputed site of the Ark. With some perseverance and luck (and more probably, Divine intervention), we were able to locate someone who could guide us to the location of the Ark formation located in the mountains of Ararat.

Barry, Jerry and Russell show their delight in arriving at the Georgia-Turkey border crossing.

Eastern Turkey is beautifully barren, as mountains and plains of sand are split by a few meandering serpentine dirt roads.

Jerry is caught in a reflective moment as he looks upon his fellow passengers and the row of hanging salamis aboard the bus at the border crossing between Georgia and Turkey.

Russell and Barry shown here with "Steffi" and friends in the hotel lobby in Ardahan prior to our interrogation by machine gun toting members of the Turkish security force.

On the morning of our departure from Ardahan, only a few hours after our two late night interrogations by authorities, the cobblestone street with our hotel shown in the left foreground is deserted.

Here we are preparing to leave from our hotel in Ardahan with our driver for the trip to Dogubayazit and the Noah's Ark site.

As we learned, when you travel the rough terrain and roads in this region of the world, the question of changing tires becomes one of when and not of if.

One of the many machine gun emplacements we saw in this troubled part of the world.

A close up view of one of many military vehicles that we saw during our journey in eastern Turkey.

Much of eastern Turkey is in a state of disrepair. Some buildings have been bombed by the skirmishing parties.

Small mosque with accompanying minaret, where muezzins call five times a day for worship.

Our driver assists us in presenting our bags for inspection at one of several checkpoints along the route to Noah's Ark.

The military presence in Eastern Turkey was more than conspicuous. Armed troops can readily be seen here out the front windshield. Lucky prayer beads are seen hanging from the rear view mirror.

Soldiers on patrol were seen throughout eastern Turkey, including on the streets of Dogubayazit. Naturally, they were well armed.

Along with the ever noticeable military presence, sheep, goats and other livestock were seen on the streets of Dogubayazit.

Led by Barry's perseverance, we went into Dogubayazit's police headquarters, though no one spoke English, and likewise, no one recognized our sketching of the Ark site.

A view of Dogubayazit with the peak of Mt. Ararat lost in a layer of clouds, as if often the case. This shot was taken from the third floor balcony of the hotel Ortadogu.

54

The new hotel Ortadogu was a refreshing sight, as rudimentary English was spoken here, which in turn led to a knowledge of the Ark location.

Shown here is Jerry's third floor room at the hotel Ortadogu. All you had to do was slide open the door to the balcony and there, majestically in front of you, was Mt. Ararat.

A view from our balcony of the street in front of our hotel, the Ortadogu, in Dogubayazit.

The afternoon markets of Dogubayazit were bustling with men and boys transacting their business. The few women we saw were traditionally covered from head to toe in spite of the 80 degree heat.

t's morning roundup time in Dogubayazit, as seen in this picture from the rear window
f the car taking us to Noah's Ark.

If a picture is worth a thousand words, this morning shot of the prominent silhouette of Mt. Ararat should perhaps be valued at ten thousand.

On our way to the Ark, we followed the road to Agri. The next day, after our exploration of the boat-like formation, we would spend the night in Erzurum.

Although we never actually saw it, we did not honestly believe the Simer was all that bad a hotel. The numerous bullet holes dotting their sign outside of Gule, Turkey, however, indicated that perhaps some may have felt otherwise.

By the morning after our stay at the hotel Ortadogu, the clouds had parted, leaving the snow capped summit of Mt. Ararat in plain, although not ordinary view.

Military traffic on the road to Nuh'n Gemesi (Noah's Ark).

Military patrol returning from the direction of Iran, only five miles from the Ark location.

A dirt and gravel road winds through the mountainous terrain to the Ark site.

Snow capped Agri Dagh (Mt. Ararat) lies in a military off-limits zone, as does the Ar formation, a scant few miles to the south.

Trip leader, Ron Leadbetter, on our way to the ark is shown smiling although he too was repeatedly roused from slumber by artillery shelling and minaret blaring.

Father and son, Jerry and Russell Lemler, share a light moment together as they head for a fantasy destination.

The "Guardian of the Ark", Hassan, is pictured here with the Visitors Center in the background.

Barry Rice is pictured with Hassan, "Guardian of the Ark". The Ark structure is shown in the background.

This spectacular view awaited us on our arrival at the site. At first, all we expected was to stand on the hillside from which this picture was taken. We were more than surprised when we were allowed to go down and walk freely on and around the Ark.

Here is another view of the Ark formation.

And another, slightly different, view of the Ark formation.

Jerry eagerly goes to explore the boat-like formation.

This photograph, taken at an altitude of 6,200 feet, looks toward 17,000 foot Mount Ararat and the surrounding countryside.

Hassan points to the bore hole of a 30 meter soil sample taken a few years ago. Testing results were reportedly inconclusive. Additional testing and investigation will be necessary when, and if, the current military situation so permits.

Vertical streaks at regular intervals are speculated by some as being evidence of the location of framing timbers of the deteriorating Ark. Near the center of the photograph is the bore hole that Hassan pointed out to us as having been made a few years before when a soil sample was taken for testing.

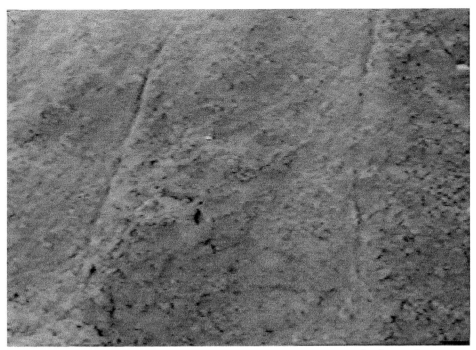

A closer view of a side wall of the Ark formation reveals longitudinal, evenly
spaced markings.

This view shows a distinction between the dark lava-crusted side wall and the light-
colored soil at the base, which reportedly fell away from the wall following an
earthquake three decades ago.

71

Here Ron is standing in the center of the Ark formation with Jerry in the background above a mountain spring.

From this angle, a downhill view, one can see the lower end of the
Ark. Mt. Ararat looms ahead.

" . . . the same day were all the fountains of the great deep broken up . . . " Genesis 7:11 KJV. A mountain spring which lies adjacent to the Ark formation is visible in the background. Jerry is shown here as he approaches the crumbling west wall of the Ark formation.

This picture shows a closer view of the exposed west wall.

This angle shows an uphill view of the pointed bow of the great ship.

A close up view of the west side of the stern of the Ark formation.

Numerous tiny, spiral seashells surround the Ark remains.

This close up of a seashell on the Ark formation is one of many that we saw in this barren eastern Turkish region. The nearest body of water is a fresh water lake, Lake Vann, which is about 50 miles away.

Barry, standing near the center of the Ark formation, takes a closer look at what is thought to be a ballast stone.

Jerry poses near one of the several stones on the Ark formation, which are believed to be ballast stones.

These stones, which are believed to be ballast stones, appear to be lined up with one another.

From this downhill view looking toward the lower end of the Ark, both Barry, near the center, and Jerry closer to the stern, are visible. Also visible are Mt. Ararat in the distance and the mountain spring closer to the Ark formation itself.

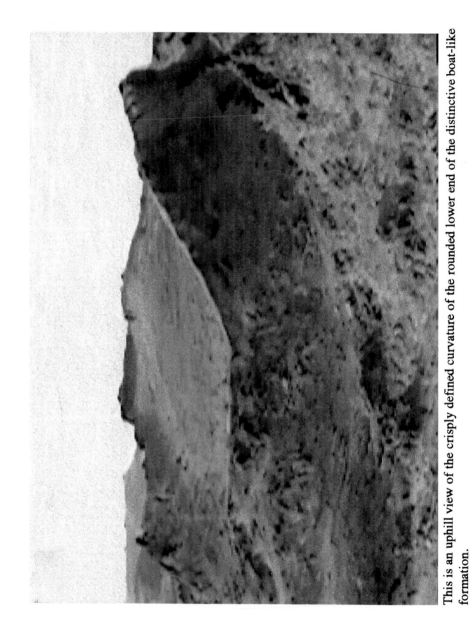

This is an uphill view of the crisply defined curvature of the rounded lower end of the distinctive boat-like formation.

Jerry is shown here with the Ark formation in the background. The exposed west wall of the Ark formation is clearly visible from this vantage point.

Barry is shown here from a slightly different angle with the Ark formation in the background. In addition to the exposed west wall, cattle, which are dwarfed by the Ark formation, are also clearly visible.

Person on top of the formation adds perspective to the colossal height of its wall.

Barry is pictured here in this view, which faces the bow of the Ark formation.

Jerry navigates the rugged volcanic terrain below the Ark formation.

View from the center of the Ark looking south toward the stern or back of the boat-like formation.

A closer view facing the bow or front of the boat-like formation.

The tiny village of Uzengili overlooks the site, and stands a stone's throw from the visitor's center.

A run-down visitor's center overlooks the site. Military conflict has for the foreseeable future put an end to tourism and excavation possibilities.

We were shocked and pleasantly surprised that we were allowed to freely handle and review the papers and drawings in the visitor's center.

Ron examines ark site drawings, certificates, photographs and newspaper articles found inside the Visitor's center as Russell looks on.

Noah's Ark or natural phenomenon?